HIS LIFE & WORK

 Evening Standard

The Mail
ON SUNDAY

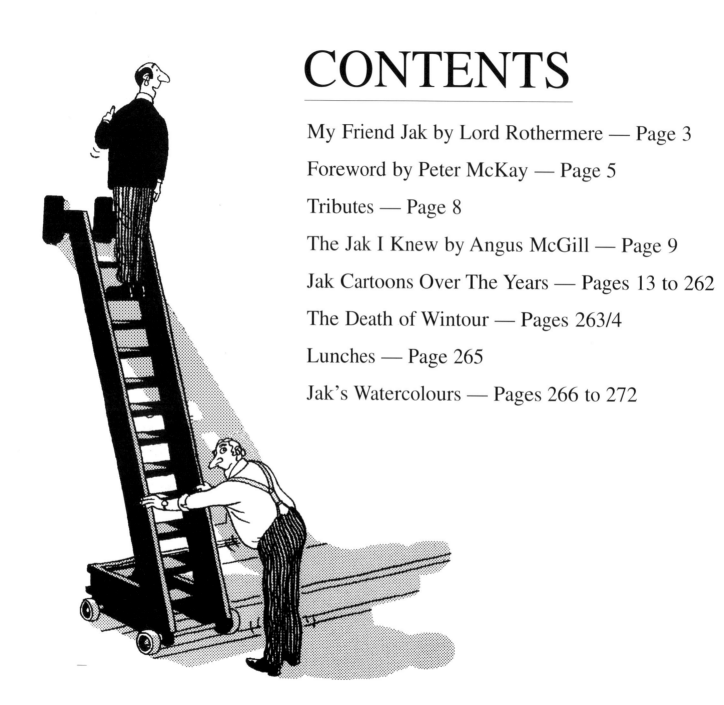

CONTENTS

MY FRIEND JAK

Lord Rothermere

UNCLE JAK, as he preferred to be called by his many friends, came into my life on the acquisition of the Evening Standard. I had admired his work for years as one of the all-time greats alongside Rowlandson, Gilray and Illingworth. I invited him to lunch. Jak, being Jak, was adamant that I be his guest. Jak's hospitality was legendary, so I happily accepted — what a lunch! The best champagne, finest burgundy and claret followed by superb brandy; the afternoon was lost in laughter and good company.

Far and away better than all this was the discovery of Jak's warm and vibrant personality and that rare thing — an unassuming and totally unspoiled genius. His was a really free spirit, a true life-enhancer to all around him, above all a man of compassion.

Jak was a determined man, and would never give up on anything. He resolved to learn golf and joined our Northcliffe Golf Society. Golf can be an infuriating game and proved very much so for Jak, but rain or shine, heat or cold, bunker or rough, pond or brook, found or lost, he never stopped. Even in the twilight one could discern his small and indomitable form pursuing his umpteenth ball down a distant fairway. Jak had balls — and he certainly needed a good supply for golf.

Jak was never boring — the unforgivable sin in journalism. One day a parcel arrived in my office. In it was the most charming and original watercolour of fishing boats in a harbour. It was signed Jak. He had painted it on holiday at his beloved villa near Cadaques on the Spanish-French border.

I was astonished. Here was a cartoonist who not only had the wit of Rowlandson but could paint as well as he. From then on, every year, one of his superb watercolours would appear in my office to be whisked off home. These are here in this commemorative book for you to enjoy.

To say that my wife, Maiko, and I miss our Uncle Jak is an understatement, for his untimely death leaves a gap in the lives not only of his loved ones but also of his dear friends and the millions who enjoyed his work and laughed with him at the foibles of mankind.

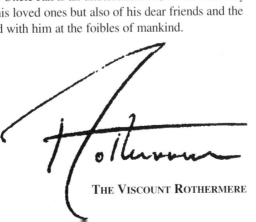

THE VISCOUNT ROTHERMERE

The life of Jak: (clockwise from bottom left) enjoying a pint of Guinness at The Cartoonist behind Fleet Street in the early Eighties; as a child in London aged about eight and two; a childhood message to mum; the aspiring artist in his twenties; on a motorbike in 1946 during his army service in Egypt; with son Patrick in 1989; Jak's Press card from 1977; enjoying the sun in Cadaques in 1997.

FOREWORD
Peter McKay

SMALL, wiry and as strong as an ox, Jak was asked by the keep-fit instructor of a gym he was joining what he hoped for in the way of body improvement. He said: 'I want to be a foot taller' — Jak had a simple, uncomplicated admiration for bigness. He'd have signed up for a frame-replacement operation if they'd promised him a six-foot-plus body. Or hung upside down for a week with weights on his ankles if he'd been told that might have the same effect. But he was big in every way except stature — in talent, in generosity and in spirit. Most of all he was big in laughter — in making others laugh and in laughing himself. Jak's great shout of laughter rang through low taverns, naughty nightclubs and even the mind-your-manners formality of the Savoy Grill.

Jak's capacity for enjoyment was enormous. He loved company more than any man I've ever known. His zest for eating, drinking and merriment never dimmed and it was infectious. Next morning, white-faced colleagues, swallowing aspirins by the water machine, would explain: "Out with Uncle Jak." Living life at full throttle was Jak's modus operandi. This was where he found his funny ideas. When he died, aged 70, a friend remarked: "Yes, but he lived 90 of them."

The cartoonist is every proper newspaper's most prized contributor, able to lift the daily torrent of news and comment on to another stylish, witty plane. It is also the hardest job of all. Editors, sub-editors, writers and photographers have all kinds of support systems. Everything they do individually can be sharpened and improved by colleagues. Cartoonists have their pens, their paper and their brains.

Each day, be it dull or historic, they must fashion from events some timely joke, draw it up and finish before the presses are ready to roll. No one can help them. They stand or fall by their own efforts. The lonely pressure is great but they must train themselves not to think about it. The perfect result — a funny cartoon, instantly understandable — always looks simple but it's a work of intense and detailed concentration.

Jak carried this burden lightly. He never agonised publicly

about the pressures. He thought of himself as a fortunate man — being paid well for work he loved — and never gave those who whined about how hard they worked the time of day. He also relished his success without ever suggesting by word or deed that it was only his due, which it was, or that it set him apart from or made him better than colleagues and friends whose efforts were more modest. Uncle Jak got on with it. No navel inspecting for him, unless the navel in question belonged to a belly dancer.

Jak was not an introspective man but he was a thoughtful one. He was interested in politics and philosophy. As a native-born Londoner, he was cynical of all politicos, wondering why (as he saw it) it was always necessary for them to lie. But he liked and admired the strong characters among them — delighting in Margaret Thatcher, regretting John Major's inability to project strength and, towards the end of his life, not having made his mind up about Tony Blair. The cover drawing for his 1987 annual shows a handbag-waving Mrs Thatcher chasing a huge crocodile back into its pool.

He was not, like his predecessor Vicky, a Labour supporter. Nor could he be said to have been a Tory one, except in the sense that he believed in self-reliance long before this was adopted as policy by New Labour. Jak didn't seek to make propaganda for any party in his political cartoons: just make people laugh by showing that politicians are as absurd as anyone else. He often portrayed them as venal, lecherous hypocrites but there was no "side" to his wit; he didn't lampoon them in the expectation or desire that it would make them any more wholesome.

Some cartoonists seek to charm us, especially on slow days, with the kind of coy drawings over which we're expected to explain: "Ah, isn't that nice?" Jak had no time for such sentimentality. He was always out to find the killer joke, the belly laugh. If his drawings seemed more hard-edged and news-related than those of some rivals, perhaps this was because he sat among Evening Standard journalists early in the morning as he read the papers and absorbed their cynical banter and gallows humour. He once captured, in all its idiocy, the long-running row over how the 180-mile-an-hour Eurotrain would have to go slower when it got on to old-fashioned English rails by drawing the massive, sleek French locomotive meeting, nose-to-nose at Dover, a Victorian tram car.

To say Jak's drawings were not politically correct is an understatement. He hadn't the faintest understanding of what the intelligentsia deemed suitable, or otherwise, as joke material. Even after newspapers began increasingly to employ serious-minded women executives who deplored gender-based jokes, Jak's cartoon ladies were outrageous stereotypes: half-naked, willing-to-canoodle sirens or bitter, old bats.

Likewise his men were either tall, impossibly handsome types or cowering, timid creatures. Often he would link snivelling little men in raincoats and flat caps with enormous, battle-axe wives. The newspaper might fulminate about the behaviour of cads but as a cartoonist Jak often took the side of reprobates. When the Duchess of York's father, Major Ronald Ferguson, was alleged to belong to a massage joint, Jak drew a number of polo ponies tethered to the railings outside the club in question.

He knew what made us laugh involuntarily, not what he thought ought to be funny. For more than 40 years he drew for the Evening Standard and (for the last 10 years) The Mail on Sunday, a prodigious output of around 10,000 drawings. His relationship with the editors who came and went was friendly but firm: each day he gave them about half a dozen roughs to choose from, and accepted without complaint the decision they made, even if they had failed to pick his favourite. But he did not welcome any further participation from them in the joke process. All he required was that they laughed and pointed to the rough that tickled them most.

Otherwise their job was to make the Evening Standard successful and well regarded. He never took any strong view about their editorial preferences. Nor did I ever hear him talk disloyally of any editor. He loved the Evening Standard unconditionally.

Jak's background wasn't posh but he bore no resentment against those who were grand, either in life or in his drawings. His upper-class characters were always drawn with fondness — great, mustachioed belted earls grasping brandy glasses in imposing libraries whose sons called Tarquin said, "I say, pater". Or gentlemen's club types in evening dress demonstrating their bafflement with modern life and news. He loved the company of military types, particularly the SAS who with him began Jak's Black Pudding Club.

His lunches with them sometimes lasted for days. These eating, drinking and merry-making forays were planned like military exercises, except that the result was often a higher level of walking-wounded than even the tough SAS might have tolerated in battle. He liked these uproarious occasions to be punctuated by increasingly incoherent speeches, appalling jokes and wild suggestions about future party venues under "any other business". I can see him now, balloon of brandy in hand, pounding the table and shouting: "Order! Order!" There was precious little order when Jak was around.

Jak in Hereford, 1993. He loved the company of military types and formed a close friendship with the Special Air Service.

TRIBUTES

On the day following Jak's death tributes poured in from close friends, colleagues and admirers of his work.

Prime Minister **Tony Blair** explained how he would feel the loss of Jak. "He will be remembered as one of the finest political cartoonists," he said. "I will greatly miss Jak's political insight."

William Hague, Conservative leader: "Jak was one of the great political cartoonists. He served the Evening Standard and Londoners for 45 years. His humour was incisive and amusing, and everything he did was a collector's item. He brightened our lives, and all of us who are politicians were teased in the right way, with artistry and humour. I am sorry to hear of his death."

Max Hastings, Editor of the Standard: "Jak was the very life and soul of the Evening Standard. He could talk to Londoners in a way that struck a chord with every one of them. He was London through and through, and, of course, possessed the genius to translate his wonderful jokes into those wonderful drawings."

Sir David English, Chairman and Editor-in-Chief of Associated Newspapers, publisher of the Evening Standard: "Jak was one of the greats, as a character as well as a cartoonist."

Lord Archer, author: "I knew Jak very well and have three of his cartoons. I really admired his work and he sold me my first cartoon for £50. He was as witty as his cartoons and he was certainly a great draftsman. Jak was among the best two or three cartoonists in Britain today and was highly respected among his peers."

Frank Dickens, creator of Bristow: "Jak was one of the finest cartoonists this century. We met at a meeting of the Cartoonists' Club at the Mucky Duck pub in Fleet Street and have been friends for 36 years. I started with the Standard and he had been doing drawings for a caravan magazine when we met. After we'd been to the pub together I would ask him the following morning if he remembered the man he was standing next to at the bar and he would draw the man from memory. He was a great bloke and was a truly remarkable talent."

Rick Brookes, cartoonist who worked with Jak for 17 years at the Evening Standard: "I feel like I have lost a brother. He was one of my best friends. We used to go to the gym together and, although he always wanted to be a foot taller, I think he was probably one of the biggest men I know."

Ron Underwood, Jak's fellow judo practitioner and family friend: "We had been friends since the Fifties and I am desolated by his death. He was a generous guy with a wonderful sense of humour. He never really grew up, but in a nice way."

Michael Heath, former Evening Standard and Sunday Times cartoonist: "He was a thoroughly wonderful man and a superb cartoonist, he just kept on sketching. When you got to know him he was so kind. His cartoons hit the mark and his death is a terrible loss."

Wally Fawkes, who drew the long-running Flook cartoon strip in the Daily Mail: "He carried on the great tradition of cartoonists started by Giles. Jak leaves a large gap."

A former officer in the **Special Air Service**, which has a collection of Jak's cartoons in its barracks in Chelsea and Hereford: "Jak was always very popular with soldiers and officers who found the cartoons hilarious. The regiment is saddened to hear of his death."

THE JAK I KNEW
Angus McGill

THERE have been three major political cartoonists in the lifetime of the oldest inhabitant and, as you might expect, all made their great reputations at the Evening Standard. First came Low, hugely serious, a man who could make or break political reputations, a power in the land. Then, after a short gap, there was Vicky, highly strung, passionately principled, personally feeling every injustice in an unjust world. Then came Jak.

Jak was nothing like the other two. They were firmly Left-wing. He was, by and large, somewhere on the Right. They were totally committed to the causes that drove them. You never quite knew what to expect from Jak. They wanted to change their readers' minds. Jak wanted to make them laugh.

From time to time a truly shocking event would provoke a serious drawing, the more effective for being rare, but for 31 years, with the news pages full of gloom and disaster, cheerfulness kept breaking out in the paper's political cartoon. When this year Jak's drawing had to stop it was the jokes that were remembered in the torrent of readers' letters. Good humour can change minds too.

Jak started life with a more usual name, Raymond Allen Jackson. At school he was a skinny, undersized kid. They called him Ray when they weren't calling him Winkle and pushing him about. He didn't care for this much and an early family snap shows him, arms like twigs, holding up dumbbells, grimly doing a bit of body building.

Jak was born in Marylebone in the heart of London, the son of a tailor, Maurice Jackson. The family was bombed out during the Blitz and moved to a nice little house in Notting Hill Gate in time for Jak to take his 11-plus. He failed. Happily there was an art test too which would get him a place at Willesden Tech at 14. He sailed through. The deal was general education until 16 and a full-time art course until 18. Then the Army got him.

He was called up at the beginning of 1945 and spent three years in Italy, Egypt and Palestine, doing, as he put it, nothing more damaging than teaching art. He was Sergeant Jackson when he was demobbed and then it was back to Willesden Art School for two years of serious training

"We had 40 years together and now I miss him every day." Jak and Claudie on their wedding day and relaxing in France in 1995.

in commercial art with the National Diploma in Design at the end of it.

That, and his outstanding student portfolio, got him a job straightaway. He was taken on as a general artist by Link House Publishing and then moved on to the richer pastures of an advertising agency where he was quite a sensation. He would arrive at work in an old taxi painted bright yellow and before long he arrived with an arm in plaster after a workout at judo the night before, just what an artist needs.

Judo had become a big thing in Jak's life. His one ambition as a boy had been to be six feet tall. He never made it. Still, though shortish, he was wiry and knew a thing or two and it was a foolish yob who picked a fight with him now. He was a member of the Budokwai Judo Club, then in Ebury Street, and was well on the way to the coveted black belt and nothing, not even a beautiful young wife alone with their baby at home, could keep him from the gym three nights a week. "It was a big bone of contention," says Claudie, his wife.

Jak had met Claudie at the Linguists Club in Kensington. She was a French au pair, just 18, who had come to London to learn English which is why *she* was there. Jak was there to meet girls. That night they went dancing at the Studio Club, a then celebrated dive behind Regent Street, and Jak drove her home to Bromley where she was working. "He was such a gentleman," says Claudie. "He opened doors for me, there were chocolates in the car, he always picked me up and took me home. I had never had that sort of attention. I thought it was lovely." So did Jak. He was in love, he sent red roses, he proposed. "Marry an Englishman?" cried Claudie, now 18½. "Never," and went back to France. "He came chasing after me," she says, "and I changed my mind."

The wedding was in Fulham Register Office with Claudie very chic in a black new-look costume made by Jak's father. Black? "As I was three months pregnant," she says, "I thought I should not wear white."

Jak, by now, was safely on the Evening Standard. He arrived in 1952 as a general artist, doing any drawing the paper needed, decorations for the TV page, illustrations for features, caricatures of people in the news, and an increasing number of pocket cartoons. It was the cartoons that launched him on his life's work.

In 1966 Vicky, in the grip of a dreadful depression, took an overdose of sleeping tablets and Jak took over. The great man's shoes were not easy to fill and the editor of the day, Charles Wintour, had hesitated. He thought Jak was too lightweight, not a political animal, but Wintour was persuaded and Jak got his chance. He took it with both hands. For the next 31 years he became an integral part of the Evening Standard.

He soon established a working style that he maintained until the end. He was a tremendously sociable man and did not want a studio of his own. He preferred to occupy a large office, half of which was his. The rest was the territory of the other artists. There he worked beside the window behind a barricade of shelves and the sloping slab of his drawing board, always sure of plenty of company. The room was known to everyone as Jak's Cabin and there were items there not to be found elsewhere on the editorial floor. A fridge was an early addition to the scene, filled with champagne. A squashy black-leather sofa arrived for his afternoon naps. A rather ramshackle bar was rigged up, the only one in the office.

Here he was to be found at 7am every day, whatever the rigours of the night before. First there were the morning papers to be read. Then, perched up on a high stool at his drawing board, he would sketch out the roughs of five or six ideas and by 9am was presenting them to the editor. There was usually at least one among them that could send them both to jail. Successive editors reacted in their respective ways. Some held their heads in their hands. One looked carefully at each rough in turn with no expression at all. Others, and these were the ones Jak liked, actually laughed from time to time, but all picked a cartoon in the end and off went Jak to his cabin to get it drawn.

This took every minute of the rest of the morning. As the hours passed Jak, now in shirt sleeves and wearing an extremely practical butcher's apron which gave him a long pocket for this and that, would be drawing, drawing, drawing. He would also be taking telephone calls, chatting with visitors, recounting his adventures of the night before, rifling around for a reference, losing his temper, finding it again, roaring with laughter, and marching to the gents to clean his teeth.

As blessed lunchtime approached the drawing would be nearing completion. Then bang it was done and off he would go, to the Savoy or the Royal Garden or Marco Pierre White's latest joint where he would be the centre of a Falstaffian company for the next three hours. "I always think of him surrounded by laughing friends, calling for champagne," wrote one such.

A short siesta on the sofa would set him up for the evening which might well last until the early hours, and then it was 7am again and he was back at his desk. He had a constitution to marvel at.

The drawings that took shape in Jak's Cabin by day over 31 years are the body of this book. Taken together, his collected works form a ribald history of our time, great events and small jostling cheek by extravagantly exaggerated jowl, each drawing populated by a wondrous *galère;* royals, politicians of every kind, assorted presidents, prime ministers, industrialists, models, rising stars, falling stars, Irish navvies, gay vicars, tarts in fishnet tights, all with only three fingers and none of them, to tell the truth, looking their best, bellies this way, noses that.

Jak had his favourites and they became stars in their own right. He loved dowager duchesses, shelf-like bosoms decked with the family jewels; Irish builders, massive hands grasping pints of Guinness; retired colonels apoplectic in front of vast fireplaces. Above all, perhaps, were the bimbos, long-legged, high-breasted, full of Western promise. Jak was quite impartial. The bimbos got off lightly but he had a go at everyone else. His victims loved it. Usually. Innocent onlookers were constantly amazed that people satirised so wickedly couldn't wait to buy the originals.

A Jak cartoon featuring your very good self became, indeed, a badge of celebrity. Do you have one in your downstairs loo? Oh dear! Never mind.

It is not known where the Queen hangs her Jak cartoons but all we can say is that several have gone to the Palace. There used to be an unwritten prohibition on caricaturing the Royal Family. Jak claimed to have been the first to break it. Was he marched to the tower? Not at all. The Queen, he found, didn't mind a bit.

One or two, though, have taken severe umbrage. Jak fielded some extremely nettled telephone calls in his day and at the height of their power the trades unions tended to bristle a lot. On one famous occasion the printing unions stopped the paper because of a Jak cartoon. It was the one he did on the power station strikers (see page 16), calling them boneheaded and worse. The power station at Tilbury demanded that Jak pay them a visit so, to all our surprise, he did, purring through the gates in his E-type Jaguar with its personalised number plate. Would he come out again? We needn't have worried. All concerned got on like a house on fire.

Jak took such things entirely in his stride but, all the same, the one thing that really got him going was any suggestion of censorship. The Evening Standard, like all grown-up newspapers, has lawyers to keep us out of trouble and sometimes they say no. When this happened to

Jak he was outraged. "Every time they stop a cartoon I want to hit them," he said. Still, they didn't stop many and, in 31 years, Jak was never sued.

One company of men who never complained was the SAS Regiment. At all times Jak couldn't wait to get abroad and he made a number of hugely successful sketching tours for the Evening Standard. They took him, among other exotic places, to Borneo where he came face to face, for the first time, with an SAS trooper. He was being tattooed by a Dyak head-hunter with a bottle of Quink. The trooper and his mates took him under their wing. He visited the tribes with them, had a wonderful time and started a close friendship with the whole regiment that lasted the rest of his life.

He started drawing the men in black after the Iranian Embassy siege and they often starred in his cartoons after that. Then the Colonel of the Regiment bought the originals for the mess and called into Jak's Cabin with the Regimental Sergeant Major to pick them up. Jak took them out to lunch. This went so well that many other lunches followed. At one of them, at the Savoy Grill, the Sergeant Major asked if they did black pudding. Certainly they did. A noble black pudding arrived and Jak's Black Pudding Luncheon Club was born. It was, and still is, a most exclusive fraternity. It has an emblem — a winged black pudding. It has a tie and a flag and just 22 members, and some of the lunches have been known to go on until the following morning. Black pudding is always served. The club continues.

Jak listed walking and golf as his sole recreations in Who's Who and he certainly spent hours walking on Wimbledon Common with the big macho dogs that he and Claudie always had — a blokish boxer, an alarming bull mastiff, a much-loved Labrador.

He had, actually, a host of other recreations, some of which I can mention. Sketching, for instance. He took watercolours with him whenever he went abroad and every holiday produced a clutch of accomplished paintings. He painted Cadeques, the little Spanish seaside town on the French border, again and again. Picasso had lived there, Salvador Dali had lived there, and Jak and Claudie had a flat on the hill overlooking the bay.

He could have added dancing. He and Claudie danced spectacularly together all their married lives. "Jiving and making love," says Claudie. "They were our two hobbies."

Making love could certainly have been added to his recreations, also living it up. His salary at the Evening Standard was legendary and he spent it lavishly. All his life he loved parties, clubs, champagne, fast cars and the company of women. He was simultaneously devoted to his family, Claudie and their three

Judo became a big thing in Jak's life. He was a member of the Budokwai Judo Club

children, Dominique, Patrick and Natalie. Natalie, the youngest, last year married an Olympic judo silver medallist. The wedding was a tremendous bash in the South of France and you never saw a happier man than the father of the bride.

Paradoxically, Jak prized the domesticity of life in the sunny house at Wimbledon where he and Claudie had lived for 38 years. He was, for instance, very keen on his lawn. Well it was a most superior lawn, rising in billiard-table terraces at the back of the house with Claudie's herbs growing happily among the flowers in the borders.

His private life, wrote one obituarist, defied analysis, which was true enough, and there were times when Claudie rebelled. She packed a bag and left him once but Jak, full of remorse, swiftly found her and they came back together, happier and more secure than ever. Her memories

are full of love and laughter. "He was a rogue," she says, "but such a lovable one. He never wanted to hurt me, I know that, but he loved to have fun and I'm proud and happy that we stayed the course. We had 40 years together and now I miss him every day."

The constitution that had been one of the wonders of our time had lately started to show signs of wear. He needed and got a new hip, stumped around the office on a stick for a while and made a wonderful recovery. Then there was trouble with his heart. He had a heart-valve operation in July and this, too, seemed a total success. Within days he was out of hospital and back home. On his last Sunday he had walked his daughter's dog on the Common as he loved to do and was sitting with Claudie in his garden on that lovely summer afternoon when she saw him slipping away.

He died, the ambulance on its way, in her arms.

"I do hope you don't come out swearing like your father!"

21 February 1970

Buckingham Palace announced that Prince Charles, then 21, would join the Royal Navy under a graduate entry scheme.

"Courage mounteth with occasion" *(Shakespeare's King John).*

15 April 1970

The seemingly doomed Apollo 13 moon mission eventually saw the spacecraft return to earth with all three astronauts alive and safe.

"Archie! — Weren't you in Calcutta?

28 June 1970

The controversial show Oh! Calcutta! was first staged in the West End to howls of disapproval.

Homo-electrical-sapiens Britannicus, circa 1970.

9 December 1970

Britain suffered its worst power cuts for years, brought on by the electricity men's work to rule. They complained bitterly at Jak's cartoon.

**"Let me put it this way,
Wilkins, can you imagine
saying 'Hello, hello, what's
going on 'ere?' in hot pants
AND kinky boots?"**

27 February 1971

The Metropolitan Police announced it would
update its women's uniforms by allowing
boots to be worn as regulation wear.

"I want that girl escorted from the Royal Enclosure within 24 hours!"

29 April 1971

A row loomed over whether women wearing hot pants would be allowed into the Royal Enclosure at Ascot. Racecourse officials ruled them OK but the Queen's representative issued a statement declaring them out.

"Now it's all over, Argyle, how about a look at the back numbers?"

6 August 1971

Prison sentences on three editors of Oz magazine unleashed a storm of controversy. Judge Argyle jailed Richard Neville for 15 months, James Anderson for 12 months and Felix Dennis for nine months.

"At least when he read the
newspaper we didn't have
to look at him as well!"

21 January 1972

Television companies were given the
go-ahead to broadcast around the clock.

"I speak to you tonight — er, by kind permission of the NUM, the ETU, the NUR, the AEW, the GMWU ...!"

22 February 1972

In a television broadcast Prime Minister Edward Heath appealed to the reasonable people of Britain to withdraw from the brink of economic disaster and to fight the forces of anarchy.

8 March 1972

Crisis loomed in Cyprus following Greek government demands that a 'Government of National Unity' be set up in Cyprus and that Czech arms imported by President Makarios be surrendered to the UN peacekeeping force.

"Never mind, Harold, you've still got us!"

11 April 1972

The Labour Party leadership split in a row over the Common Market and three Cabinet Ministers, including deputy leader Roy Jenkins, resigned.

"There must be some way I
can programme it to say
'Yes' to my Vietnam
policy!"

9 May 1972

President Nixon ordered a sea blockade of
North Vietnam and the bombing of her rail
links with China.

"It's either an awfully progressive school, or a protest about school uniforms!"

20 May 1972

London witnessed a demonstration of pupil power when thousands of children walked out of school and went on the march. They were demanding a greater say in the running of their schools.

"... altimeter, pressure gauge, port engine trimmer — and back there registers the rise in costs!"

2 June 1972

It was revealed that the Anglo-French Concorde cost £21.5 million for each plane compared with the £3.5 million estimated when the project began 10 years earlier.

"A forgery? Haven't you seen one of the new floating pounds before?"

26 June 1972

Britain set the pound free to find its own level against other currencies worldwide.

"I'm afraid I've got to ask you to take your knickers off!"

7 July 1972

The debate over tobacco sponsorship in sport began in earnest.

"What happens if Iceland extends its territorial waters again?"

9 August 1972

The Shell group discovered a major oilfield i the North Sea. At the same time Britain and Iceland continued to dispute territorial waters.

"We're here to investigate allegations that this prison is too soft!"

25 August 1972

Angry prison officers demanded a special conference to discuss lack of discipline inside Britain's jails.

Another Arab gold medal for cowardice.

6 September 1972

Arab guerrillas attacked the Israeli team's quarters at the Olympic Games in Munich, killing two team members. Further Israeli hostages later died during a bid to rescue them.

"I know it was a landslide victory, Dick, but ...!"

9 November 1972

President Richard Nixon won a spectacular election victory, crushing his opponent, Senator George McGovern. Nixon's win invaded all the historic sanctums of the Democratic Party and shook the landscape of American politics with one of the greatest landslides in US history.

"A pint of Euro-bitter, a small Euro-gin and lime and two packets of Euro-crisps!"

3 January 1973

After centuries of bad blood with Europe 55 million Britons became Common Marketeers.

24 January 1973

President Nixon told the world that America had achieved "peace with honour" as a ceasefire agreement was signed in Paris. More than 1.5 million civilians and soldiers had died. The Vietnam war was over.

"One day, my son, all this will be in Japan!"

20 February 1973

Shop stewards representing 50,000 Ford workers voted for a total strike over their pay claim.

"I think it's something to do with this new motorway box thing!"

21 February 1973

The Government approved "in principle" a box-shaped motorway circling inner London. Known as Ringway One, it was never built. Ringway Three was eventually the choice — today's M25.

"Your bill, gentlemen — now shall we start to haggle about VAT?"

8 March 1973

In the Budget Chancellor Anthony Barber fixed VAT at 10 per cent — lower than the previous purchase tax. Ice-cream, sweets and soft drinks were surprise VAT exemptions.

Hear nowt! See nowt! Say nowt!

16 March 1973

There were no signs of an end to the crippling rail and gas strikes and hospital workers and teachers both rejected pay offers. Prime Minister Harold Wilson refused to intervene.

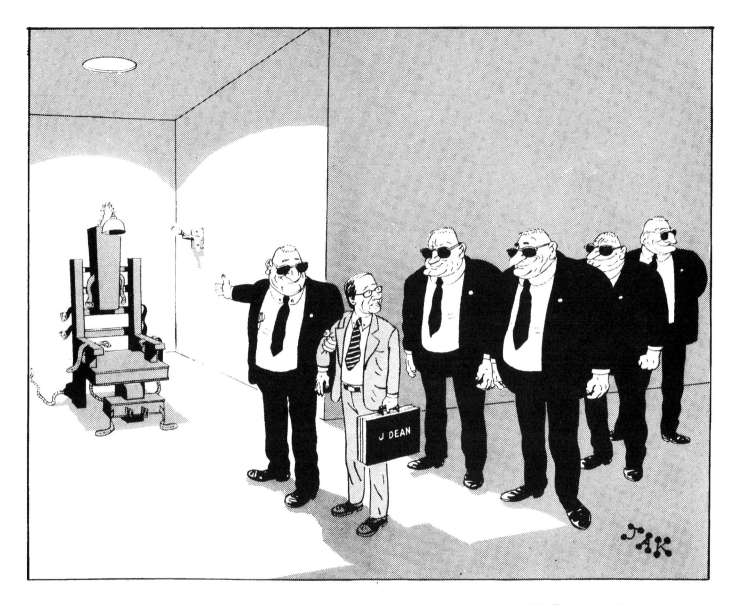

"Are you sure it's a lie detector?"

28 June 1973

John Dean, the former White House counsel, told Senate investigators that President Nixon had discussed with him every aspect of the Watergate cover-up.

"Now, before we sing the hymn Dyma Gariad Fel Y Moroedd, let us offer up prayers for Richard and Liz!"

6 July 1973

Elizabeth Taylor announced her decision to separate from husband Richard Burton after a nine-year marriage. She blamed his return to drinking a year after he had signed the pledge.

" ... and for the next couple of days, keep your eyes open for any Press photographers trying to sneak in!"

12 November 1973

Fleet Street eagerly awaited the marriage of Princess Anne to Captain Mark Phillips.

"Can you get it through to that snivelling, idle, half-witted son of ours that Ted Heath is not going to force him to do three days' work a week?"

17 December 1973

Prime Minister Edward Heath announced there would be a three-day working week in most shops, offices and factories from 1 January.

"There is absolutely no truth in the rumour of a shortage of toilet paper in Britain!"

14 February 1974

"Can I put you down as a militant don't know?"

22 February 1974

The nation prepared for a General Election and, as usual, all eyes were on the opinion polls.

"... and forgive me all the fibs I've told, and all the promises I've made...!"

28 February 1974

Edward Heath, Harold Wilson and Jeremy Thorpe prayed as the electorate went to the polls.

"Seems Enoch will do anything to get back to Westminster!"

22 April 1974

The stage was set for the possible return to the Commons of Enoch Powell as an Ulster Unionist. Meanwhile a rugby international at Twickenham was interrupted by a famous streaker.

"I cannot tell a lie — I didn't do it!"

7 August 1974

President Nixon at last admitted he knew about the "political implications" of the Watergate scandal. He resigned the next day.

"If you think the coq au vin is a bit underdone, wait until you see the steak au poivre!"

1 November 1974

Six leading London hotels were hit by a 48-hour strike by chefs, chambermaids, porters and waiters.

"And now to advise us on survival in a harsh economic climate ...!"

14 July 1975

Prime Minister Harold Wilson announced tough anti-inflation plans, including limiting all pay rises to a maximum of £6.

"Nothing personal, Reg, but we feel you don't project the right image for Newham North East Labour Party!"

21 July 1975

Overseas Development Minister Reg Prentice struggled against the Left wing in his constituency. He eventually defected to the Tories.

**"But I am smiling,
Margaret!"**

10 October 1975

Mrs Thatcher became leader of the
Conservative Party but was publicly snubbed
by former leader Edward Heath at the party's
annual conference.

"Would it be discriminating to enquire which PERSON is picking up the bill?"

30 December 1975

The Sex Discrimination Act came into force.

"CAUGHT YOU!"

18 March, 1976

Harold Wilson resigned. But who would be
his successor?

His Master's Voice ...

8 April 1976

Jim Callaghan defeated Michael Foot by 176 votes to 137 in the ballot for the leadership of the Labour Party. Meanwhile, the unions maintained a firm grip on government action.

"Codpeace in our time!"

3 June 1976

Foreign Secretary Anthony Crosland
announced the end of the "Cod War".

"All right, all right! We'll get air conditioning!"

29 June 1976

Britain sweltered in the hottest summer of the century.

"Good news, Mr Healey, we've stopped the pound falling!"

29 September 1976

The value of the pound dived to an all-time low against other major currencies. Foreign-exchange dealers lost confidence in sterling. One said: "It's not a question of a crash — just a steady, unstoppable descent to Hell."

"Denis — I think the IMF terms have arrived!"

29 November 1976

Cabinet Ministers awaited details of the terms for a £2,400 million International Monetary Fund loan to Britain.

"Under defence cuts, Wilkins, guess who's going to be our total commitment to Nato?"

15 December 1976

Chancellor Denis Healey announced defence cuts totalling £100 million.

"Don't listen to it, dear, if it upsets you!"

14 March 1977

England's cricketers faced overwhelming defeat in the Centenary Test against Australia in Melbourne. The poor state of English cricket was a favourite target for Jak and inspired many cartoons during his career.

"It's tasteful, understated, factual — I like it!"

23 March 1977

Tory leader Margaret Thatcher challenged Prime Minister James Callaghan by submitting a motion of 'no confidence' to the Commons. She said of the Government: "There is not a man or woman of principle left in it."

"I notice Kojak is still using a Buick!"

22 April 1977

American car bosses and motorists were furious when President Jimmy Carter brought in bigger taxes on fuel.

"If you think that was funny, wait till it gets to the bit where Marcia tells Harold what to do!"

30 July 1977

Sir Harold Wilson claimed that British security men had "bugged" 10 Downing Street while he was Prime Minister.

"What do you want first, the good news or the bad news?"

23 August 1977

The travel plans of more than a million airline passengers were thrown into confusion when Britain's air-traffic-control assistants voted overwhelmingly to start an all-out strike.

"Usual story, can't get a plane home, family haven't eaten for three days ...!"

31 August 1977

The walkout by air-traffic-control assistants left many travellers stranded.

"Harry can beat that. He gave up jogging, not smoking and not drinking in four minutes 23 seconds!"

3 January 1978

New Year resolutions to keep fit were, in some circles, short-lived.

"Well, you should strap the over-forties to their seats!"

23 March 1978

Saturday Night Fever hit London as the movie, starring John Travolta, filled cinemas all over the capital.

"The first six rows will represent Mick, and the last six rows, Bianca!"

17 May 1978

The impending divorce between Mick and Bianca Jagger looked set to become a messy legal battle.

27 September 1978

Ford car workers yet again threatened strike action over pay..The Winter of Discontent loomed.

"It's another disillusioned Labour voter!"

11 October 1978

Unions failed to adhere to the five per cent pay code as Tory leader Mrs Thatcher called on Labour voters to think again before backing Jim Callaghan for another term in office.

"I've never known negotiations this tough before!"

2 November 1978

There seemed to be no end to the strike of Ford car workers. Union negotiators turned down the Ford company's offer of nearly 15 per cent — three times the Government limit at the time — and voted to extend the strike into its seventh week.

"I still say the management are bluffing!"

27 November 1978

Under threat from The Times management to close down the newspaper, last-minute attempts were being made to get an agreement, but the National Graphical Association refused to negotiate.

2 Jan 1979

The new year got off to a grim start with the whole of Britain under snow for the first time since 1963. Hundreds of motorists were trapped in drifts.

"Let them eat cake!"

9 January 1979

While Britain was suffering mounting chaos — lorry drivers on strike, train drivers threatening to join them, petrol unobtainable and housewives pack-buying in face of the siege — the Prime Minister, Jim Callaghan, was in no hurry to return from the Guadeloupe summit. In fact he went on to Barbados.

"No, we don't get much secondary picketing around here!"

22 January 1979

The industrial turmoil got even worse with threatened strikes by public services — including schools, hospitals, municipal airports, rubbish collectors and cemetery workers. And the big issue was secondary picketing — groups of workers not involved in the strike forming picket lines to prevent lorries moving.

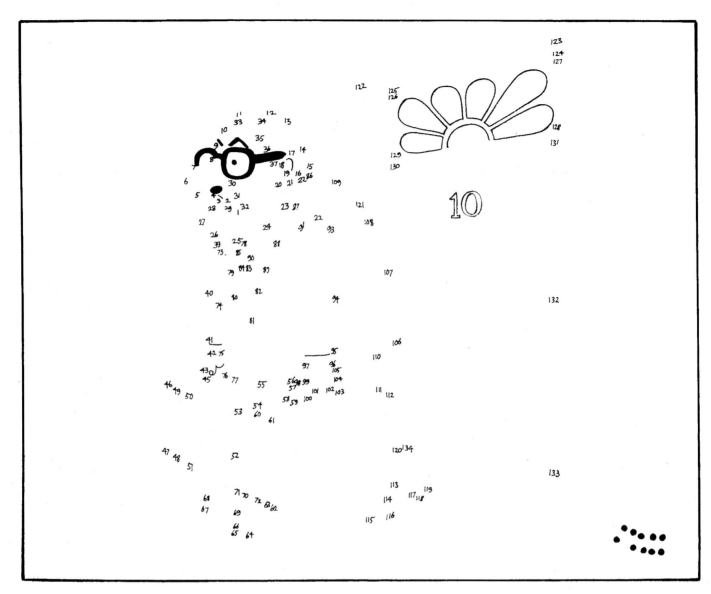

Jak is on strike too. Draw it yourself.

24 January 1979

London was shivering and wet and almost everything was on strike. Jak decided that he'd had enough misery. He joined what seemed to be the mood of the moment and offered this cartoon to readers.

"We'll have to stop meeting like this, Gwyneth — they've put a tachograph in my cab."

7 March 1979

The European Court ordered Britain to comply with Common Market law that all freight lorries carry a tachograph — known as the "spy in the cab". The government reluctantly acquiesced.

"No, McClory, you can't turn Protestant 'just for the Pope's visit'!"

1 August 1979

There was mounting excitement about the Pope's projected trip to Ireland, and there were hints that the Irish Roman Catholic hierarchy would be calling for a ban on alcohol during the visit.

"M'Laird, could ye ask the party to unload before we give them the week's bill?"

15 August 1979

The grouse season opened amid reports that there was hardly any game to shoot anywhere. The shortage was put down to the hard winter, but hunt saboteurs were out in force to frighten the birds away.

"I must insist on the lady juror in the front row removing her funny mask and water wings!"

12 September 1979

A man, about to be sworn in as a juror in Croydon County Court, suddenly put on a horror mask of a wrinkled old man with a big nose. The judge ordered him to the cells for a few hours and fined him £50 on his return.

"It broke down on the way!"

15 October 1979

Sir Michael Edwardes, chairman of British Leyland, gave the unions an ultimatum: "Agree to the axing of 25,000 jobs, closure of 13 plants, or BL can go to the wall."

"Alas Monsieur, ever since the Evening Standard victory, the customers have demanded English wine waiters!"

30 October 1979

Who knows more about wine, the British or the French? The Evening Standard challenged the Paris newspaper Le Figaro to a contest and the Standard wine team won hands down.

"I may not know much about art, but I'm married and I've been cleared by MI5!"

20 November 1979

One of the greatest spy scandals in years was uncovered when it was revealed that Sir Anthony Blunt, the 72-year-old former adviser on art to the Queen, was the "fourth man" who helped spies Burgess and Maclean to flee Britain in 1951. Blunt was one of a coterie of homosexual spies.

"No, this won't be the airport, just the main runway!"

18 December 1979

The Government finally announced that the site of London's third airport would be Stansted after all.

"It's mainly local trade around here, sir!"

22 January 1980

A newspaper alleged that prisoners at Sudbury Open Prison, Derbyshire, were being offered visits to a prostitute for £200, a night out with the wives for £100, and were able to buy drink and drugs.

"I say, Denis, have you seen this awful drawing of me?"

31 January 1980

A caricature of Mrs Thatcher to be used by the Labour Party in a drive to recruit new members was unveiled by Eric Heffer. It made the Prime Minister look like a cross between a witch and a vulture.

"'Ello, 'ello, what's going on 'ere?"

23 February 1980

More than 500 British policemen were flown out to Zimbabwe (then Rhodesia) to help supervise elections. The police were all volunteers, carried no firearms and had no power to arrest.

"Naturally, this cottage is twice the normal price because of its unique location!"

10 March 1980

English-owned houses and cottages in Wales were going up in flames with monotonous regularity. Welsh Nationalists were suspected.

"Attention à votre derrière, Gaston!"

3 April 1980

French and Belgian farmers invaded London to protest against the ban on liquid-milk imports. The demonstrators brought a Normandy "cow" with them and tried to give away pints of French milk.

"Rodney never uses the front door since he joined the SAS!"

6 May 1980

A six-day siege at the Iranian Embassy in London ended when an SAS squad stormed the building and brought out all the remaining hostages. Only two terrorists survived the action. The gunmen who had seized the building had demanded the release of political prisoners in Iran's Khuzestan province.

"Game to Borg and Co!"

25 May 1980

Wimbledon time and could anyone beat Bjorn Borg, the champion who stood to earn millions from sponsors if he won the title again? (He did!)

Poles apart!

8 December 1980

The first of a series of threats for a military invasion of Poland came from the Russians as the difficulties with the recently formed trade union, Solidarity, reached crisis point. The Russian Army newspaper warned: "The joint armed forces of the Warsaw Pact will guarantee the continuation of Communist rule in Poland."

"You passed on two, Mastermind — you don't go past Luton when you come from Heathrow and 15 from 20 leaves five!"

23 December 1980

Fred Housego, a London taxi driver with only one O-level, outwitted all opponents to become Mastermind of 1980 in the BBC TV contest.

"Yours I think Charles?"

6 January 1981

Some of the Royal Family were getting irked by the antics of press photographers who were hoping to get a glimpse of Prince Charles with Lady Diana Spencer. At Sandringham he walked over to a group of them and said: "I wish you all a happy New Year — and your editors a particularly nasty one." His brother, Prince Andrew, warned a photographer watching a pheasant shoot: "Don't stand there — you could get hurt."

"On no account is he to hear any more cricket news!"

19 February 1981

The England cricket team faced obliteration against the West Indies in the first Test in the steamy tropical heat of Trinidad. They scored only 178 in their first innings in answer to the West Indies' first-innings total of 426 for nine declared, and had to follow on.

"The Dean would like a word with you!"

5 March 1981

Everyone was trying to cash in on the Royal Wedding, and it was reported that souvenirs worth more than £100 million were being manufactured for sale to an eager British public. Among the items were mugs and plates, jewellery, headscarves, pictures, books, postcards and toys.

"The usual, Winston?"

14 April 1981

In a weekend of rioting and violence, mostly by black Londoners on the streets of Brixton, 161 policemen were hurt, 121 people were arrested, 26 buildings were destroyed (including several pubs) and damage ran into millions of pounds.

"WHAT'S THIS EAR?"

25 April 1981

Top jockey Lester Piggott had to have a 45-minute emergency operation to save the top half of his right ear which was torn off at Epsom when his mount, Winsor Boy, panicked in the starting stalls.

"Eighty-six years ago Oscar Wilde got sent to prison for it, 14 years ago it was made legal, under Ken Livingstone it's going to be compulsory!"

20 August 1981

Ken Livingstone, controversial leader of the GLC, pledged his support to gay-rights groups and alleged that police and Army chiefs were planning a Right-wing coup in which the victims would be "gays, trade union activists and Left-wing politicians".

"I've got a complaint to make about one of your heat-seeking missiles."

21 August 1981

Two Libyan aircraft were shot down by US fighters after a clash off the North African coast where the US Sixth Fleet were engaged in naval exercises. The US and Libya blamed each other for the incident.

"Personally, I think they've been on honeymoon far too long!"

19 October 1981

Princess Diana, it was reported (and denied), had a shot at a stag and had only succeeded in wounding it. The League Against Cruel Sports became very indignant about this.

"I didn't think that applied to *your* own mother, Raymond!"

9 November 1981

Suddenly everybody was interested in the royal baby on the way ... but who could blame a pub landlord for taking a strong line?

"It beats me how we ever got along without the Falklands for the last 150 years!"

20 April 1982

A thought that may have occurred to many a neutral (not necessarily pacifist) observer.

"Well, I heard the British
SAS were all about this
size!"

24 April 1982

Argentinian troops dug in for the expected
British counter-attack — and there were
doubts about the morale of Galtieri's finest.

"I suppose you'll be putting this down on your expenses!"

26 April 1982

Three British journalists were held by the Argentinians on spying charges — they were taking notes, which is of course always something suspicious for a reporter to do — and Jak shrewdly saw the financial possibilities in the situation.

"You worry about world opinion, I'll worry about the commandos!"

17 May 1982

Some Argentinian troops, not madly enthusiastic about the forthcoming encounter, might have been happy to seize on this notion by Jak of how to disengage with honour.

"Right, gentlemen! How many of you can slide 80ft down a rope from a helicopter?"

18 May 1982

Occasionally relations between troops and press became strained and no doubt some NCOs would have been glad to see some reporters at the sharp end. The redoubtable Max Hastings, who may be recognised in Jak's line-up, was the first man into Port Stanley.

"I don't know what effect it's having on the Argies but the 2nd Paras have pulled back 25 miles!"

5 June 1982

The British counter-offensive against the Argentinians took various forms ...

**"We didn't have a flagpole
so we used Max Hastings!"**

16 June 1982

Not only was Max Hastings a very successful
Falklands correspondent, he was also a very
tall one.

"Did you have a corrupt day at the office, dear?"

24 July 1982

There was a rash of stories in the press that implied that not all policemen were honest Jack Warner above-suspicion types — a few found ways of supplementing their incomes.

29 October 1982

This cartoon appeared after an outbreak of sectarian killings and violence in Northern Ireland — the Commission for Racial Equality did not condemn it but a full meeting of the Labour-controlled Greater London Council called the cartoon "racist" and decided to stop advertising in The Evening Standard as a protest.

"Bejesus Mary! Did you ever see Murphy do O'Connell Street in 35 seconds before?"

11 February 1983

Shergar, the 1981 Derby winner, was kidnapped from his stable in the Irish republic.

**"It only seems like
yesterday we were all in
the cabinet office
answering Mrs T back!"**

13 June 1983

A cabinet reshuffle — and some Tory
ministers found themselves back in the
ranks …

"I think he's doing a World Exclusive interview for The Sun!"

9 August 1983

The Sun newspaper admitted that an "interview" they had with the widow of a Falklands hero awarded the Victoria Cross was fabricated.

"Finally, Norman, I'd like you to take a little test!"

18 October 1983

Norman Tebbit took over from Cecil Parkinson at the Department of Trade and Industry.

"Mum! Dad! You can come in now. The video nasty's finished!"

25 November 1983

A survey alleged that an alarmingly high percentage of young children had seen video nasties.

"They say the wheelchair chase is fantastic!"

14 December 1983

Sean Connery, not in the first flush of youth, returned to active screen duty as Agent 007. Few could have predicted his seemingly everlasting sex appeal.

"A train set! A train set! You'll have a ****** computer like everyone else!"

24 December 1983

The day Father Christmas met an old-fashioned child …

Did you hear the joke about the Irish lorry driver who nearly fooled the French?

9 February 1984

French farmers were holding up foreign meat lorries in yet another protest.

"I'm afraid you've left it a bit late for the duty-free shop, sir!"

10 February 1984

Some British residents were being taken out of war-ravaged Beirut by car ferry.

"Next!"

29 February 1984

At the Government Communications HQ, Cheltenham, the deadline was set for obeying the Government's order to give up union membership and take the £1,000 offered.

122

"... And finally, have you noticed any change in Harold since he started watching video nasties?"

9 March 1984

An official report confirmed the high number of children who had seen videos not meant for their impressionable little minds ...

"Too noisy at the Iranian Embassy! Too cold in the Falklands! Sometimes I wonder why you lot joined the SAS!"

26 March 1984

The Queen began a royal tour of Jordan amid strict security.

"He was gasping for a fag!"

22 June 1984

Smoking was to be banned completely on the
London Underground.

"Surely you knew the punishment for killing sheep in Roehampton?"

25 September 1984

An Iranian diplomat slaughtered a sheep in a Roehampton street, to the outrage of local people. He claimed diplomatic immunity.

"See the vicar? I am the vicar!"

16 November 1984

The Church of England Synod voted to move towards the ordination of women.

"You fired the entire sales department, broke Mr Wilkins's arm, promoted the doorman to vice-chairman and proposed to the cleaning lady!"

27 December 1984

The Christmas party was over ...

"I thought they worked by computer!"

16 January 1985

The controversial Sinclair C5 electrical vehicle was launched.

**"Every time he gets drunk
he gets another one done!"**

23 January 1985

Some European Parliament members — not
the British — suggested that cats and dogs
should have identity numbers tattooed on
their ears.

**"You bloody fool! The
Shah of Persia's been dead
for years!"**

12 April 1985

Ambitious newspaper publisher Eddie Shah
secured an impressive loan.

"Your mother and I made just one mistake on VE-day, Tarquin — and you're it!"

8 May 1985

Nostalgia time, 40 years on ...

"Now, with this piece of high-tech robotic engineering you won't need anybody at Wapping!"

30 January 1986

The blessings of new technology were becoming increasingly apparent

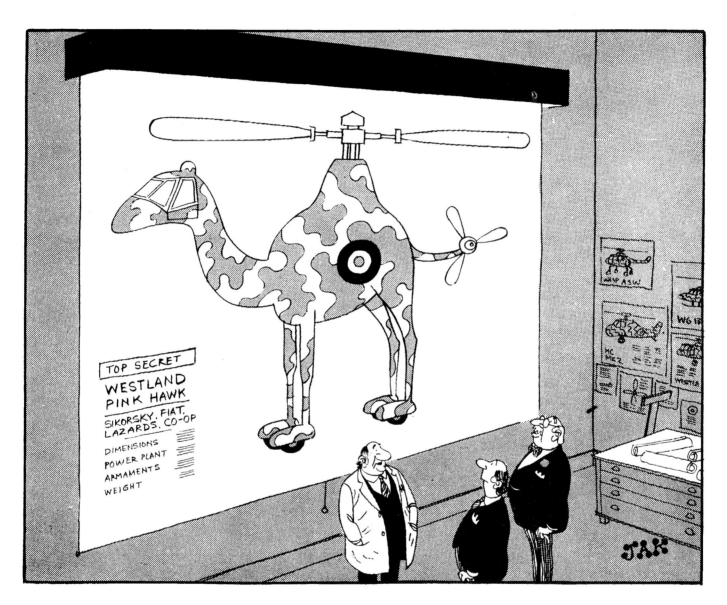

"It was designed by a select committee!"

13 February 1986

Westland shareholders voted overwhelmingly for the Sikorsky-Fiat bid.

"Tactically, do we lodge our appeal to him for a raise now, or after the honeymoon?"

3 March 1986

Lord Hailsham married the woman who had been his secretary 40 years before. Meanwhile, barristers were pressing him over their pay claim.

"The manager's compliments, and if you don't put a bet on in the next hour he's going to break both your legs!"

11 March 1986

New-look betting shops, with food and drink, carpets and colour TV, opened.

"I hope you don't mind, but I've been longing to use my bus pass."

22 April 1986

During a State visit by the King and Queen of Spain, Queen Elizabeth celebrated her 60th birthday.

"I wish you'd tell us when you're burning your stubble, we've just evacuated Birmingham!"

12 May 1986

After the Chernobyl disaster, drifting smoke clouds were worrying.

"Watch out which button you press for the lift!"

27 May 1986

The new Lloyd's building, rather like the Pompidou centre in Paris, was opened in London.

"...and we can dump it in New York for only £99 a load!"

2 June 1986

Mrs Thatcher asked Richard Branson to lead a campaign to make Britain a litter-free zone.

"Hello! Marks and Spencer? Just to confirm your order of two dozen pairs of navy blue knickers for Mrs Thatcher!"

22 August 1986

Mrs Thatcher revealed that she bought her underwear at Marks and Spencer.

10 October 1986

Haringey Council ruled that Baa Baa Black
Sheep should become Baa Baa Green Sheep.

"Personally, I like it — but we'll have to see what the Commissioner thinks!"

2 December 1986

Some people complained about explicit sex scenes in Dennis Potter's "The Singing Detective" series on TV.

"I'm looking forward to the food hall!"

15 December 1986

Sir John Sainsbury, chairman of the supermarket chain, is to become chairman of the Royal Opera House.

"You could use them for all sorts of things!"

19 December 1986

Boeing's AWACS early-warning radar system had been chosen in preference to the British (GEC) Nimrod…

"The next time you call a recruit 'a mummy's boy', find out who his mummy is!"

8 January 1987

Prince Edward, not enjoying the Royal Marines officer training course, was wondering whether to stay on…

"You should get a gold medal for that in this weather, young man!"

14 January 1987

Britain was in the grip of its coldest weather for years.

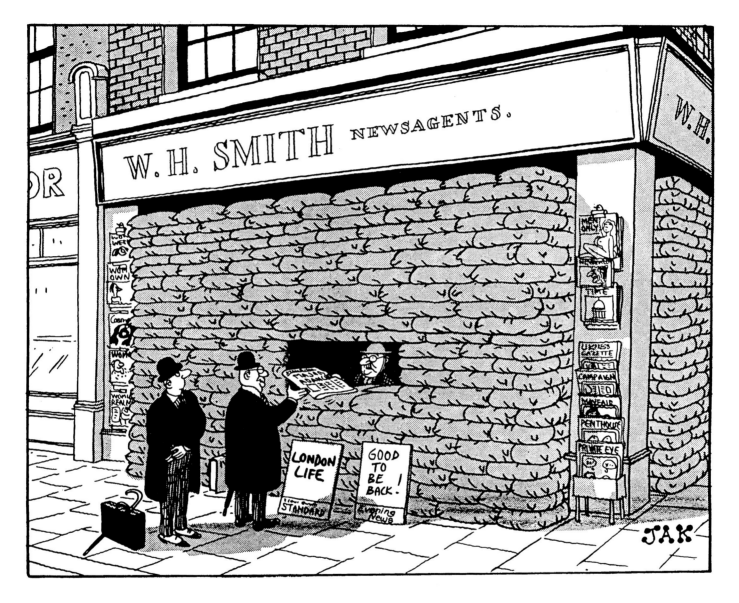

"Don't you know there's a war on?"

25 February 1987

On the day that the London Daily News appeared, Lord Rothermere re-launched the Evening News as a stablemate for the Standard.

"Hello! Luscious Linda here! I'm wearing a thick woolly vest and gum boots ... for further titillation put another 10p in!"

9 September 1987

For 38 pence a minute you could pass on sexy messages, all part of British Telecom's services.

"Is there any other business?"

29 September 1987

Europe won the Ryder Cup golf contest in America for the first time.

"Have they gone yet?"

12 October 1987

The fascination of the Loch Ness monster ... a sonar scan investigated the length of the loch to no avail.

"This could be our best day ever!"

19 October 1987

Hurricane-force winds brought down thousands of trees in London and the South-East.

"Jackson's beginning to show signs of stress!"

27 October 1987

Shares were plummeting worldwide ...

"...And the matchstick!"

29 January 1988

Westminster City Council were behind a
scheme to recruit ex-servicemen and former
police personnel for an anti-litter campaign.

"Well done, Eddie, you've broken the British record!"

16 February 1988

Britain's Eddie Edwards achieved fame by finishing last in the Winter Olympics ski jumping.

"Polo ponies! I thought it was the Household Cavalry on Tuesdays!"

10 May 1988

Major Ronald Ferguson, the Duchess of York's father, was alleged to have been a regular client at a massage parlour.

**"It was all the excuse
Henry needed to avoid
water completely!"**

13 June 1988

A report linked aluminium in water to
Alzheimer's disease.

"Of course he's smiling, he just tasted his first private postman!"

1 September 1988

Postmen went on strike over a scheme for bonus payments in London and the South-East, and private delivery firms prepared for a boom.

"Well, see what Alexander Walker thinks of the Texas Chain-Saw Massacre!"

7 September 1988

A film about Great Train Robber Buster Edwards was criticised for being too sympathetic to criminals.

"Any more for barbecued dove?"

19 September 1988

Scores of doves were incinerated when the Olympic flame was lit at Seoul.

"...Manny Cohen's doing well in bespoke tailoring, Monty Stein's gone bankrupt in Beirut, Issy Bloom's opened another business in the wife's name, Mrs Shapiro's son's Bar Mitzvah is at the Connaught Rooms, Harry Goldman ring your mother...!"

21 September 1988

Israel put its first satellite into space.

"You won't find any cockroaches here, mate, the rats eat 'em all!"

24 November 1988

The Dorchester hotel was fined for having dirty kitchens. Cockroaches were found under a fridge.

"Ah, Bertie, have you met my offspring? Rover, Spot and Lassie."

19 January 1989

During a Lords debate on capital punishment, one peer suggested children should be thrashed like dogs.

**"Who did they mistake
Nigel Benn for this time?"**

27 January 1989

Police hunting a suspect mistakenly issued a "wanted" picture of boxer Nigel Benn, who then knocked out the man who tried to arrest him.

"I don't care what the police say, I feel a lot safer on the Tube with the Guardian Angels!"

31 January 1989

Leaders of New York's Guardian Angels were trying to set up a similar organisation in London.

"Now if diddums isn't a very good boy and wins a lot of prizes, diddums is going to end up on an RSPCA poster!"

12 February 1989

The RSPCA issued a shock poster featuring a pile of dead dogs.

"We think you've picked the wrong disguise, Salman!"

16 February 1989

At the same time as Salman Rushdie was hiding from avenging Moslems, the Sun offered a £1 million reward to find Elvis Presley, who was said to have been spotted all over the place.

5 May 1989

Mrs Thatcher was celebrating a decade in power.

"Come on, Mavis, I bet Mrs Thatcher doesn't moan about 30,000 volts!"

21 May 1989

The Prime Minister spoke of the relaxing benefits of a special bath that passed a mild electric current through the water.

7 June 1989

The Chinese army slaughtered thousands of students protesting peacefully in Tiananmen Square, Peking.

"Roger and I are engaged. Would you like to see the strawberry?"

29 June 1989

Wimbledon's traditional strawberries were working out at about 40p each. After a public outcry the prices were reduced.

**FRENCH REVOLUTION
SPECIAL**

10 July 1989

It was 200 years since the French Revolution
and "JAKQUES" helped the Evening
Standard celebrate with a special edition.

"Sent down from Harrow! Cashiered from the Guards! Deserted from the Foreign Legion! It's going to be damned difficult getting you into my club, Peregrine!"

10 September 1989

Hundreds of English soccer fans were arrested after going on the rampage in Stockholm.

"Would you call dinner with the Bishop an acid house party, dear?"

24 October 1989

Police turned hundreds of would-be acid house partygoers away from motorway services.

"Hey, Jimmy! Can you spare a fiver for a wee drop of Chateau Latour '59?"

7 January 1990

Glasgow was European City of Culture 1990. Would this change things?

"It's an Australian Crocweiler"

8 March 1990

After concerns about rottweilers and pit bull terriers, what could possibly outscare the new "horror" dog, the Bandog?

"And finally, a two-minute silence for Councillors Snodgrass, Wilkins and Smedley, who went down so gallantly during the anti poll tax protest!"

12 March 1990

Throughout the country council meetings were violently disrupted by protestors as the members tried to set the level of the new poll tax.

"Did the earth move for you too, Gwyneth?"

4 April 1990

A minor earthquake, centred on Wrexham, rattled homes all over the country.

"But, Edward, you don't have to prove yourself to me, I'm your mother!"

11 April 1990

Prince Edward told the Daily Mirror he was tired of people thinking he was gay.

"Look, Dad, it's one of those French trains."

17 June 1990

The Government refused to fund a high-speed rail link between the Channel Tunnel and London. Critics claimed the slower journey would damage Britain's trade.

"I do hope you're not going to come home from your club in that state every night!"

27 June 1990

The IRA blew up the Carlton Club in St James's, injuring eight people.

"Mildred and I were just admiring those wonderful friezes on the gate of the Herculaneum when we were seized by the Carabinieri for some reason or other!"

1 July 1990

The World Cup authorities in Italy deported 247 England fans for hooliganism, although many claimed they were innocent bystanders.

"Where were you on the night of 4th July between 6.30 and 10pm?"

5 July 1990

Thirty million TV viewers watched England lose to Germany in the World Cup semi-final.

"Relax guys, it was Shultz's socks again!"

13 August 1990

There were fears that Iraq would again resort to chemical weapons.

"What with my budget being so tight, and then just standing there doing nothing...!"

17 October 1990

According to a report on royal spending, the Queen's annual laundry bill was £63,700.

"Never mind the fine, Arthur, just take his name and address!"

30 October 1990

British Rail said they were introducing on-the-spot fines for fare dodgers.

"They all wore grey suits!"

22 November 1990

Mrs Thatcher resigned.

"We wouldn't dream of smacking Wayne, we'd sneak up behind him with a 12lb sledge-hammer!"

13 December 1990

Esther Rantzen was behind a national campaign to stop people smacking their children.

Now it begins

17 January 1991

Overnight the first bombing raids on Baghdad had started. The battle to liberate Kuwait was on.

"To Elmer J Hackenbecker, the only American to fly to London since the Gulf war…"

1 February 1991

Nervous US holidaymakers were keeping well away from Britain.

"This ticket is three days out of date!"

21 February 1991

For the second day running, hundreds of Underground passengers were trapped on the Central Line for six hours after smoke was seen billowing from a train.

"Which was the one that bit you, Mummy?"

6 March 1991

The Queen needed stitches after being bitten by a corgi when she tried to break up a fight between the royal dogs.

"Just tell him it's the Chief Whip with a complaint about the rent!"

15 April 1991

According to the News of the World, while Chancellor Norman Lamont was living at 11 Downing Street, his home was being rented by sex therapist Sara Dale, who charged £90 a go for lessons in sado-masochism in Mr Lamont's basement.

"My waiting list has been cut down dramatically since I changed my name to Hannibal!"

3 June 1991

The film Silence of the Lambs, starring Anthony Hopkins as the psychotic killer Dr Hannibal Lecter, was terrifying cinema audiences throughout the country.

"I know the zoo's closing,
darling, but why couldn't
you bring back a gerbil,
like the neighbours?"

15 June 1991

London Zoo was under threat of closure
because of money troubles.

"Put your money away Gertie, he's not a ticket tout!"

25 June 1991

Torrential rain washed out Wimbledon.

"... and now to the rousing tune of The British Grenadiers, the massed bands of the Brigade of Guards ..."

11 July 1991

Massive cuts in the size of the Army were announced by Tom King, the Minister of Defence.

"Here's another one who didn't read the new regulations properly!"

12 August 1991

New rules were introduced to force owners to muzzle so-called danger dogs when they were in public places.

"I really think you're worrying too much about these army cuts, Charles!"

15 October 1991

Just how far would the proposed cuts in military spending go?

"If you only could sing, Vera!"

13 November 1991

Madonna lived up to her reputation as pop's material girl when she clinched an estimated billion-dollar deal with entertainment and publishing giant Time-Warner.

"I 'ad a postcard once, one of those dirty ones from Brighton!"

21 November 1991

After Terry Waite was released by his Lebanese captors he talked of receiving a postcard from someone he did not know, depicting John Bunyon in Bedford Jail. This, he said, helped give him strength to endure his capture.

"I don't think it's another harvest festival, Doris. It's the vicar competing with Tesco's!"

28 November 1991

A group of supermarket chains announced they were going to flout Sunday trading laws by opening seven days a week during the run-up to Christmas.

"It's about your sexist attitude, Valerie. Now you've upset the scaffolders!"

31 December 1991

Building-site workers were threatened with the sack if they indulged in sexist pastimes, like wolf-whistling at passing women and sticking up posters of nude women.

"That's one of the colonel in the '91 Gulf War!"

16 January 1992

Some were dismayed at paintings of the Gulf War by Britain's official war artist. Two works showed Mickey Mouse sitting on a lavatory amid the horrors of war in Kuwait.

"The hunt's ready to move out, m'dear. Do you feel calm enough to face the saboteurs yet?"

15 February 1992

The Duchess of York was reputedly treated by a clairvoyant who asked her to sit under a glass pyramid designed to relieve stress while treating her for back and neck pain.

"Care for an operation, sir?"

6 March 1992

New trust hospitals set out to reduce waiting times for patients by cutting our bureaucratic wrangling and lengthy consultations.

"Tyson in solitary again"

7 May 1992

Former world heavyweight boxing champion
Mike Tyson, serving a six-year sentence for
rape, was said to have threatened prison
wardens, saying he would "whip your asses".

"As I suspected, alopecia!"   **28 May 1992**

A hitman posing as a doctor in a white coat shot and killed patient Graeme Woodhatch at the Royal Free Hospital. Unfortunately doctors did not realise he had been shot four times and the bullet wounds were only noticed when he was in the mortuary five and a half hours after his death.

**"It's this year's group
photo for Lloyd's Names!"**

5 June 1992

Huge insurance losses at Lloyd's meant that
its Names would have to foot the bill —
estimates showed that Names would have to
find an average of more than £60,000 each.

"When Howard said he was going to rescue something from the Zoo, I thought it would be more cuddly"

21 June 1992

London Zoo was threatened with closure.

"Don't throw it away, Albert, it could be von Ribbentrop or somebody!"

7 July 1992

A bizarre claim that Hitler's bones — plus those of his wife Eva Braun, propaganda minister Josef Goebbels and his wife and six children — had been found near Magdeberg in eastern Germany was written off by historians as yet another Hitler hoax.

"...and here's a secret recording of what is believed to be Bertrand Russell chatting to the Queen Mother on the telephone."

26 August 1992

Mystery surrounded extracts published from a 20-minute tape claiming to be an intimate conversation between Princess Diana and a male friend.

"Could I seek asylum for a minute? I'm desperate for a Gitanes!"

2 November 1992

France's 12 million smokers found themselves treated as outcasts in public as they were banned from lighting up in all banks and public offices. Bars and restaurants were told to provide non-smoking areas and three-quarters of train carriages became non-smoking.

"Escargots are off! Coq au vin's off! Bouillabaisse's off! Cassoulet's off...!"

9 November 1992

The US government attacked Jacques Delors' role in the collapse of the GATT talks. Acting Secretary of State Lawrence Eagleburger accused the EC commission president of "pulling the rug out" from under agricultural commissioner Ray MacSharry during talks in Chicago aimed at breaking the deadlock over farm subsidies.

"Honestly, Judith, it was bad enough when you just used to nag me!"

13 November 1992

The Church of England was on the brink of the greatest upheaval in its history. More than 450 years of tradition were overturned when the Church's parliament, the General Synod, opened the doors to the ordination of women.

"I think I've won the
national lottery, dear.
Does one shout bingo or
something?"

20 December 1992

The dream of winning £1 million on a 50p lottery ticket came
closer to reality when Heritage Secretary Peter Brooke
formally presented a Bill to the Commons to create a national
lottery to raise up to £4 billion a year for the arts, charities
and sport, and to protect art treasures.

"The Emirs couldn't afford it, but hang on, here comes someone from Lambeth Council!"

25 January 1993

A report revealed that corruption and malpractice had cost Lambeth Council up to £15 million. Labour-run Lambeth had the country's highest poll tax at £425.

"There was no need to dress for the captain's table, Miss Whiplash. Everything on the *Canberra* is terribly informal!"

26 January 1993

Following her faked disappearance, self-styled Miss Whiplash, Lindi St Clair, was found relaxing on the liner *Canberra*. At the time police were still searching for her in England after finding her Jaguar abandoned at Beachy Head.

"Sterling! Ten to the pound!"

2 February

The pound plunged on world currency markets.

Six suggestions for the Australian Republic stamps

26 February 1993

Paul Keating, the Australian prime minister, officially committed his Labour party to a referendum on making Australia a federal republic.

"Angus! Will ye get on the fax to the Americans and tell them they're dropping a wee bit short of Sarajevo!"

2 March 1993

The US Air Force prepared for a second aid drop over Bosnia after the first appeared to have missed its target. A radio ham in the besieged mountain enclave of Cerska said none of the 30 crates of food and medical supplies from the initial drop had been found.

"Hang on, old boy, I think it's your wife waving the recall flag!"

6 April 1993

Grand National starter Captain Keith Brown spoke of his embarrassment after the chaos of the race that wasn't.

Building a Greater Serbia   **15 April 1993**

Serb military chiefs came under unprecedented attack from
the UN following the bombardment of Srebenica. The town
was described as "hell on earth" and the patience of UN
officials snapped after seeing the slaughter.

"...This is Kate Adie, from the *News at Ten* battlefield!"

28 June 1993

Peak-time television news was set to change dramatically with a planned reshuffle of presenters on BBC bulletins and a new early-evening slot for ITV's main news programme, *News at Ten* — a decision that was eventually overruled.

"Very well, Edward, but you'd better let me tell your father who's going to be best man!"

21 December 1993

It emerged that Prince Edward had fallen in love with 28-year-old attractive blonde, Sophie Rhys-Jones. They had known each other for three months. But Royal aides were swift to caution against speculation of an imminent engagement. Meanwhile, Mr Blobby fever raged throughout Britain.

"It's the in-flight entertainment!"

13 January 1994

Battle lines were drawn in the Channel crossing war. It was revealed that Chunnel trains would whisk motorists between England and France for about the same price as ferries, but in under half the time. The announcement signalled a ferocious advertising war; the ferry companies emphasised the benefits of restaurants, shops and leisure facilities, while Chunnel operators pointed to speed and reliability.

"Well I didn't know he hadn't got his third star in the Michelin Guide!"

31 January 1994

Resentment that had been simmering in Britain's finest kitchens for years boiled over with the publication of the 1994 Michelin Guide. Several of the country's best-known chefs accused the celebrated guide of culinary chauvinism that ignored some of the best of British cooking. Britain has two three-star restaurants while France has 19.

"Did I hear the division bell?"

21 February 1994

The string of Tory scandals, culminating in the resignation of Hartley Booth, the Finchley MP who confessed to a close friendship with his former researcher, turned John Major's back-to-basics campaign into something of a joke.

"Fantastic redundancy figures, Wilkins. There's only you and me left — and you're fired!"

25 February 1994

Profits at National Westminster Bank enjoyed a 169 per cent lift, to £989 million. NatWest also announced that it planned 4,200 job cuts in 1994. Staff numbers had fallen by 17,500 from their peak of 109,000 in 1989, said the bank. More than 3,800 jobs were axed and 130 branches were closed in 1993.

"We'll all sit tight here, something's bound to turn up to save us!"

28 March 1994

A team of Army climbers were snatched from a treacherous gully called the Place of Death after three weeks in a cave on Mount Kinabalu in Borneo. A helicopter spotted the letters SOS picked out in white pebbles against the black backdrop of the mountain. They were not the only people in need of rescue.

"...Vera Lynn singing 'There'll be blue birds over the white cliffs of Dover' or a D-Day kissogram girl?"

18 April 1994

D-Day veterans throughout Britain pondered over ways of celebrating the forthcoming anniversary. Brewers poured cold water on a Government suggestion that beer prices should be cut on 6 June to the D-Day level of 1s 1d a pint (about 5p). An independent brewer said: "We might be persuaded if the Government reduced excise duty to 1944 levels first."

"Fascinating! Did you grow it yourself!"

25 May 1994

The fierce row over claims of dirty work in the flower beds continued at the Chelsea Flower Show. The diehards, led by John Metcalf, insisted that all the blooms should have been planted and grown by their exhibitors and poured scorn on those who imported boxes by the truckload to impress judges.

"Are you sure you'll recognise him after all these years, maman?"

6 June 1994

As the D-Day veterans returned to the Normandy beaches a warm welcome awaited most of them.

"Fantastic news, m'dear. It's a £1 million IOU from Lloyd's of London!"

6 October 1994

Thousands of Lloyd's investors took the first step to being saved from ruin after winning £504 million damages in the largest case of its kind in British legal history. But the Names were expected to have trouble collecting the millions they won as some of the defendants — the investors' agents — had already gone bust.

"No, it's not that finger.
Guess again!"

18 November 1994

The "giant finger" advertising campaign for
the National Lottery hit full steam.

"Go easy with your mother, Simpson!"

22 January 1995

Police defended their actions after smashing a blockade aimed at halting a shipment of lambs at Brightlingsea, Essex. More than 500 local residents tried to stop a convoy of four lorries by staging a sit-in across the single road leading to the dock but were moved aside by 250 officers in riot gear.

"I can't remember which one I paid to ask a question, but it looks like I've wasted my money!"

6 February 1995

The row over political sleaze took a dramatic turn when members of the House of Lords were accused of taking cash to ask Parliamentary questions. A leading Liberal Democrat lawyer, Lord Lester, rocked Westminster with a claim that four peers — as well as several MPs — had been paid to promote commercial interests in Parliament.

"Really? I've always wanted to meet a financial journalist!"

23 March 1995

The deputy governor of the Bank of England resigned after becoming the latest husband revealed as a liar and a cheat. Rupert Pennant-Rea told American journalist Mary Ellen Synon that he only married his third wife because she was pregnant and he had no alternative.

"Should have warned you I'd be late, darling, but I couldn't remember our new telephone number!"

19 April 1995

Phone codes in Britain were changed — but most only had the addition of one digit.

"I'm terribly sorry, but we don't have a leader at the moment. Could you come back Tuesday week?"

26 June 1995

John Major roared his defiance at Tory critics when he stood down from his post as leader of the Conservatives. This was a huge political gamble, challenging his enemies to "put up or shut up" — a gamble that worked.

"As the Church has banned the hymn Jerusalem, we will instead sing that well-known gay anthem, YMCA. I'm sure you all know the words!"

19 May 1996

One of England's best-loved hymns became the centre of a dispute. Jerusalem smacked of privilege, said Canon Donald Gray, the Speaker's chaplain at St Margaret's, Westminster. Meanwhile, the Church continued to grapple with the issue of gay clergy.

"Well it hasn't made much difference to my Sid, we've got 13 kids and I'm expecting again!"

28 May 1996

Doctors and parents rounded on the Ministry of Agriculture for refusing to name brands of baby milk containing potentially dangerous levels of "gender-bending" chemicals.

"You don't have to resign, Colin, you'll make a strapping WPc!"

31 May 1996

Pc Bob Reeve, a Kent village policeman who retired after 23 years in the force, regularly strolled around Tenterden, Kent, dressed as a woman. Pc Reeve said he preferred to be known as "Robyn" or Ms Reeve.

"Whatever you do, Helga, don't mention the shoot-out!"

28 June 1996

England's Euro 96 dreams were cruelly shattered by defeat at the hands of the old enemy. The nation willed Terry Venables's side to victory, but Germany won a heart-stopping and heartbreaking penalty shoot-out.

"I don't have an ID card. Will this do?"

23 August 1996

Home Secretary Michael Howard unveiled plans for a new national identity card after winning a Cabinet battle to include the Union Flag on the document.

"She gets all his money in the final scene!"

26 September 1996

Clint Eastwood settled his legal battle with former lover Sondra Locke, paying her £7 million. The movie star agreed a last-minute deal to avoid a financial hammering from a Los Angeles jury, which had already decided he had defrauded the actress.

"It seems like only yesterday I was potty-training HRH Prince Charles!"

8 October 1996

Lieutenant Commander Richard Aylard was forced out of his job as Prince Charles's private secretary because Downing Street and Buckingham Palace believed he had become a detrimental and misguided influence on the heir to the throne.

"Ah, Charles. Could you do something about that Cornish Cheese you can't sell?"

25 October 1996

Cheeses sold by Prince Charles's Duchy Originals company failed to find favour with some of Britain's finest food shops. The food hall at Selfridges stopped stocking the organically produced Single Gloucester with Herbs or Single Gloucester with Herbs and Garlic.

"Now take your time, Madam, and just point to the officer who was using bad language."

27 October 1996

A wounded policeman who swore at robbers who shot him was reported for using bad language. As unarmed Pc Clive Norman lay bleeding after being hit by a burst of fire from a sub-machine gun, he shouted: "My leg, my leg. You f****** b*****ds." A woman passer-by made a complaint to the police about the swearing.

"Apart from her blue eyes and blonde hair, nurse Hakennin held the Finnish weightlifting record for 10 years!"

29 November 1996

Black Labour MP Diane Abbott attacked her local hospital for employing "blonde, blue-eyed" Finnish nurses. She said the nurses had probably never met, "let alone touched", a black person before arriving in Britain and hinted they were not suited to work in a multi-cultural community.

"Well, I'm afraid your brain has certainly shrunk, Mr Jackson — the logical next step is a pregnancy test."

12 January 1997

Research at a London medical school showed that mothers-to-be complaining of bad memory and poor co-ordination had brains that shrank slightly during the late stages of pregnancy.

"I thought it was all over when the fat lady sings!"

19 February 1997

The celebrated Three Tenors were all found to have lovers young enough to be their daughters.

"Old Hargreaves was such a gem I had him cloned!"

2 March 1997

It was revealed that human clones could, in theory, be born in less than two years, according to the scientist who led the work to produce Dolly the cloned sheep.

"I think Channel 5 is better tonight, Pam, I can see one of the Spice Girls!"

1 April 1997

The full extent of Channel 5's reception problems started to become clear. The station's chief executive admitted that at least 40 per cent of viewers had only a fuzzy screen or were experiencing bad reception.

"No thanks, I think I'll go home with a pill."

9 April 1997

Scientists announced the discovery of a chemical called a neuro-peptide that is released in the spinal cord during sexual stimulation. This, they said, could lead to an orgasm pill.

"I don't know what the journalists are on, but could they pass some down here?"

18 April 1997

Novelist Will Self was sacked as a writer at the Observer after allegations that he took drugs in the lavatory on board the Prime Minister's campaign plane.

**"I see Peter Mandelson got
the job he wanted!"**

6 May 1997

Peter Mandelson, architect of Labour's
successful election campaign, was put in
charge of the co-ordination and presentation
of Government policy in the Cabinet Office.

"All right, Jackson, try another six with your reading glasses on!"

16 May 1997

Many police marksmen couldn't shoot straight under pressure, an internal investigation revealed. They missed completely in two out of three cases and in 13 per cent of incidents they shot the wrong person.

258

"I can't wait for Labour to ban this sport. I don't think I can stand much more!"

18 June 1997

Labour MP Mike Foster rebelled against senior party managers and announced that he would introduce a bill which could see hunting banned.

"Look out, Monica! It's the BBC knicker inspectors!"

27 June 1997

The BBC decided to draw a veil of modesty over women tennis players and their undergarments in coverage of Wimbledon.

"Now you've got charisma and gravitas, Gordon, Peter Mandelson thinks the final touch ..."

4 July 1997

Chancellor Gordon Brown's first Budget was hailed as both tough and generous, and he looked every inch New Labour personified. But there were those in the Labour Party who might have liked to see an end to his bachelorhood.

"One day, my boy, all this will be yours!"

During the Seventies and early Eighties Jak became increasingly angry about the stranglehold the print unions had over the newspaper industry. Demarcation and restrictive practices dominated Fleet Street as the unions became more militant and editors more frustrated. Jak's cartoon vision of the future — reproduced here from the original by kind permission of former Evening Standard assistant editor Marius Pope — came true. However, it was not the print unions alone who brought the demise of Fleet Street as Britain's centre of newspaper publishing. The rise of new technology and the determination of publishers to bring down costs heralded the break-up of Fleet Street as new offices and print works were found. The unions fought hard, at Wapping and elsewhere, but the tide had turned ...

When Charles Wintour stood down as editor of the Evening Standard in 1977 to become managing director of the Daily Express, Jak spent 36 hours creating this cartoon masterpiece. He called it the Death of Wintour, based on West's Death of Nelson. It features 35 caricatures of Charles Wintour's former colleagues at the Standard, including several who still work at the paper.

1	Charles Wintour	19	Former Diary editor Jeremy Deedes
2	Editor Simon Jenkins	20	Deputy Sports editor Ernie Sands
3	News editor Stuart Kuttner	21	Deputy Features editor Dick Garrett
4	Picture editor Andrew Harvey	22	Londoner's Diary writer Emma Soames
5	Sub-editor Ted Simpson	23	Travel editor Tom Pocock
6	Assistant editor Marius Pope	24	Crime reporter John Stevens
7	Sports editor Michael Herd	25	Features sub-editor Richard Bruton
8	Political editor Robert Carvel	26	Former deputy editor Roy Wright
9	Leader writer Martin Wainwright	27	Features writer Valerie Grove
10	Executive editor David Henshall	28	Arts editor Sydney Edwards
11	Cartoonist Frank Dickens	29	Film critic Alexander Walker
12	Assistant to the editor Cyril Raper	30	Columnist Angus McGill
13	Theatre critic Milton Shulman;	31	Features editor Trevor Grove
14	Splash sub-editor Bill Sharp	32	Motoring Correspondent Ian Morton
15	Managing editor Robbie Addison	33	Londoner's Diary editor Max Hastings
16	Jak	34	City editor David Malbert
17	TV Guide compiler Celia Brayfield	35	Literary editor Anthony Hern
18	Former Diary editor Paul Callan		

THE DEATH OF WINTOUR

LUNCHES

WHEN I first came to work at the Evening Standard, the cartoonist Jak took me out to lunch, an experience from which my liver took weeks to recover. We were unlikely friends, but I felt extremely fond of him over the years we knew each other, and his death was a dreadful shock, even though one knew that his heart was weak. (The circumstances of his first warning tremor were characteristically indelicate, and relayed in his inimitably ribald way.) Much has been said already about his capacity for hard work. How he managed to be at his drawing-board every day at 7am, given the way he lived, I shall never know.

There was fundamentally something rather innocent about his idea of a good time — when on the razzle, he behaved like a squaddie on 48 hours' leave rather than as the grand old man of the Evening Standard.

His punctiliously drawn and hilarious cartoons have been part of our inner lives as Londoners for 30 years.

He is simply irreplaceable.

The "on leave" image was perhaps true — perhaps why he loved the company of soldiers.

Having survived the Blitz and a pretty ropey childhood, he could never quite believe his luck. Hence the air of riotous whoopee which surrounded him. Many journalists have aspired to be legends in their own lunchtime, but few have regularly made the lunch last into the small hours of the following day. Dear old Jak.

A.N. WILSON

"Uncle Jak's" legendary lunches always required serious advance preparation and a supportive relay team to get him home.

Murdoch MacLennan
Managing Director
Associated Newspapers Limited

JAK'S WATERCOLOURS

Jak produced a newspaper cartoon six days a week for more than 30 years. He was both funny and a draughtsman. But his passion when on holiday was to paint. Here is a small selection of his work. They were painted in Portugal, Jak's beloved Cadaques in Spain, Kenya and Turkey. These watercolours are reproduced here by kind permission of Jak's wife Claudie and Lord Rothermere.

P 2050 C
SOL NASCENTE

Povoa de Varzim
Portugal 88

JAK

Cadaqués in May 1995.

House of Salvador
Dali Port Lligat
JAK '96

JAK Peponi, Lamu Island
Kenya 1992

Kharamanlar 5
Kekova Island, Turkey
JAK '93.

First published 30 October 1997

All rights reserved. No part of this publication
may be produced, stored in a retrieval system or
transmitted in any form or by any means,
electrically, mechanically, photocopying,
recording or otherwise, without writing to the
publisher for prior permission.

British Library Cataloguing in Publication Data.

Published in Great Britain for Associated
Newspapers Ltd by Solo Books Ltd, 49-53
Kensington High Street, London W8 5ED.

ISBN No 1 873939 10 8 (hard cover)

1 873939 05 1 (soft cover)

© Associated Newspapers Ltd 1997

HIS LIFE & WORK

was produced by Solo Books Ltd
for Associated Newspapers Ltd

Publishing Director: **Simon Dyson**

Editor: **Steve Pryer**

Design: **John Hill**

Graphics: **Steve Latibeaudiere**

Typesetting and page make-up: **Sally Blackmore**

Scanning and colour reproduction: **Orthodoxos Theodoulou**

Research and archive: **Douglas London**

Editorial research: **Kate Wilkins**

Consultant publisher: **Don Short**

Printing and binding: **Integrated Colour Editions Europe Ltd**

Thanks also to Clare Baldwin, Chris Locke, Tony Ward, Doug Wills, and, most of all,
to Jak's wife Claudie, without whose help this book could not have been published.